CLOSE-UP

OUR BODIES

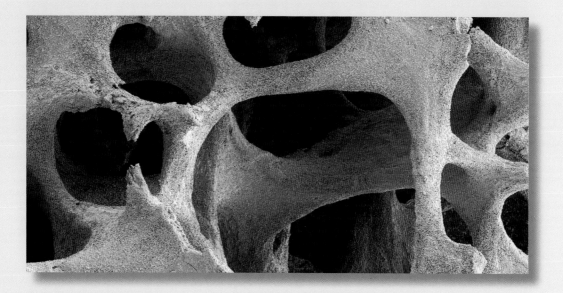

BROWN
BEAR
BOOKS

Published by Brown Bear Books Limited

An imprint of
The Brown Reference Group plc
68 Topstone Road
Redding
Connecticut
06896
USA
www.brownreference.com

ISBN: 978-1-93383-417-7

Authors: John Woodward and Leon Gray
Designer: Lynne Lennon
Picture Researcher: Rupert Palmer
Managing Editor: Bridget Giles
Production Director: Alastair Gourlay
Children's Publisher: Anne O'Daly

Picture credits
Front cover: Science Photo Library: Susumu Nishinaga
Title page: Science Photo Library; Steve Gshmeissner
Science Photo Library: Mike Agliolo 29, Eye of Science 17, 25, Steve Gshmeissner
9, 11, 15, 21, Professors P. M. Motta, K. R. Porter, & P. M. Andrews 5, 27,
Susumu Nishinaga 19, Omikron 13, David Scharf 7, Andrew Syred 23.

Library of Congress Cataloging-in-Publication Data

Our bodies.

    p. cm. – (Close-up)

Includes index.

ISBN-13: 978-1-933834-17-7 (alk. paper)

  1. Body, Human–Juvenile literature. I. Brown Bear Books (Firm) II.
Title. III. Series.

QM26.O9774 2007

612–dc22

2006103054

Printed in China
9 8 7 6 5 4 3 2 1

Contents

Hair Today

The human body is covered with hair. Most people have hair on their head. As adults, hair grows on other parts ot the body, such as under the arms. Each hair grows from a root under the skin. The root pushes the hair out of the skin through a tube called a follicle. By the time the hair grows out of the skin, it is hard and springy.

Hair Record

The longest hair ever measured belonged to a Chinese woman called Xie Qiuping. In 2004, a single hair on her head measured more than 18 feet (5.5 meters) long.

Hair facts

Human hair grows slowly. A single hair may grow up to 5 inches (13 centimeters) in a year. The hair rarely grows more than 30 inches (60 centimeters) long. It usually falls out after three to five years.

Here, hairs sprout from the dry, flaky skin on a person's head. The main purpose of our hair is to keep the body warm.

Bloodsuckers

Some insects feed by sucking blood from bigger animals. The head louse lives in human hair and feeds on our blood. It uses its biting mouthparts to suck blood from the head. The bite does not hurt. It just causes itchy spots on the head.

Catching lice

Children often catch lice from each other as they play. The lice crawl from one child to another. Female lice lay eggs that stick tightly to the hair. You must use a special shampoo and a fine-toothed comb to get rid of the lice and their eggs.

Lousy Election

People from a town in Sweden once used a head louse to choose their mayor. The men who wanted to be mayor sat down with their beards resting on a table. A louse in the middle of the table crawled onto a beard and that man became mayor.

This female head louse has laid an egg on a human hair. The egg sticks to the hair and is very difficult to remove. The female will lay up to 100 eggs during her lifetime.

Sweat It Out

When your body gets too hot, it does not work very well. People get hot when the weather is hot or when they play sport. To cool down, glands in the skin produce drops of salty water called sweat. The sweat passes through sweat pores and onto the surface of the skin.

Hot And Spicy

It may seem strange but drinking hot drinks and eating spicy foods help keep people cool in very hot places. The hot liquid and spices make people sweat. The sweat then cools the body as it evaporates from the skin.

Cooling sweat

When sweat lies on the skin surface, it evaporates (turns into gas). This uses up heat from the body and cools us down. Hot, wet weather is more uncomfortable than hot, dry weather. If the air is moist, the sweat cannot evaporate quickly enough.

A sweat pore brings sweat from a sweat gland to the skin's surface. The sweat evaporates (turns to gas), using up heat and keeping the body cool.

Skin Deep

Skin is the outer covering of the human body. It is very important. Your skin stops dirt and germs from getting inside your body. It also helps keep your body warm in cold places and cool in hot places.

Skin layers

Skin is made of layers. The outer layer is tough and stretchy to protect the body. This outer layer is always flaking away. Dead flakes drift away, taking dirt and germs with them. The inner layer has hair roots, sweat glands, blood vessels, and nerves.

Turning To Dust

The body sheds the outer layer of dead skin cells as tiny flakes. Every person loses about 1 million flakes of skin every 40 minutes. The flakes float in the air and finally land as household dust.

Human skin has two main layers. The upper layer (pink) of dead cells protects the inner layer of living skin (red and yellow).

Tasteful Tongues

The tongue is a very sensitive part of the body. It is covered with tiny bumps called papillae. There are two types of papillae—small and big. Small papillae help us feel the texture of food; for example, whether it is smooth or crunchy. The small papillae also form a rough surface that helps break down food in the mouth.

Taste Zones

Different parts of the tongue respond to different tastes in different ways. The tip of the tongue senses sweet tastes. Salty tastes are tasted just behind the tip. The sides of the tongue sense sour tastes. The back of the tongue senses bitter tastes.

Tasting food

The big papillae help people taste food. Each big papilla contains up to 200 taste buds within a ring-shaped hollow. Taste buds can tell the difference between sweet, salty, sour, and bitter tastes.

The tongue is covered with tiny papillae. The large papillae (pink) help us taste our food. The small papillae (blue) help us sense the texture of food.

Spongy Bones

Your bones support your body. The bones of a growing child are solid. As the child grows into an adult, the bones become partly hollow. The hollow spaces are filled with marrow. Red blood cells are made in bone marrow. Red blood cells carry oxygen around the body.

Hollow bones

The hollow bones of an adult are light, but they can still support the body. Branching supports inside the bone make it hard and strong. The supports make the inside of the bone look like a sponge.

Baby Bones

A baby is born with more than 300 bones in its body. As the baby grows up, some of the bones join up. By the time the child becomes an adult, the body will contain around 200 bones. Most of these bones are in the feet and hands.

The bones of an adult human contain hollow spaces filled with marrow. The branching supports keep the bone strong without making it too heavy.

Virus Attack

Viruses are tiny particles. They are parasites, which means they cannot live on their own. Instead, they live inside the bodies of animals or plants. Many viruses cause harmful diseases, such as the common cold, measles, mumps, and polio. Some viruses can even kill the animals or plants in which they live.

Virus Vaccines

When a virus attacks the body, it is often hard to treat the disease it causes. Viruses live inside the body's cells, so they can only be killed by destroying the cells. Vaccines are the best way to stop viruses from attacking the body. The vaccine helps the body destroy viruses before they attack any cells.

Cell killers

Viruses work by attacking the cells of their animal or plant hosts. One virus particle may enter a cell and force it to make more virus particles. The cell then bursts, and the viruses flood the body, ready to attack new cells.

16

A virus (red and green) attacks a cell (brown). These viruses cause a deadly disease called acquired immune deficiency syndrome (AIDS).

Personal Power

The human body needs a steady supply of food to keep working properly. Our bodies run on glucose, which is a type of sugar. Glucose comes from our food. The body also needs oxygen, which comes from the air we breathe into our lungs.

Transport system

Our blood carries glucose and oxygen to every part of the body. Glucose dissolves in a liquid called blood plasma. Red blood cells carry the oxygen around the body. The oxygen changes the glucose into energy that powers the body.

Blue Blood

The color of blood shows how much oxygen is in it. When red blood cells pick up oxygen in the lungs, the blood turns bright red. When this oxygen is used up, the blood turns dark blue.

Red blood cells are flat, disk-shaped cells that carry oxygen around our body. They also carry waste gases to the lungs, where the gases are removed as we breathe out.

A Close Shave

The hair on the top of your head grows about one hundredth of an inch (0.25 millimeters) every day. It would take a few weeks before you could tell the difference in length. The hairs on a man's face grow just as slowly. If the hairs are dark, you might see new growth in a day or two.

Longest Beard

The longest beard ever recorded belonged to Hans Langseth of Norway. When Langseth died in 1927, his beard was more than 17 feet (5.3 meters) long. His beard is now on display at the Smithsonian Institution in Washington, D.C.

Shaving

Some men grow face hair. The hair growth is called a beard. Others shave the hairs using a sharp metal razor or an electric shaver. Shaving with a razor gives cleanly cut hairs. Hairs shaved with an electric razor look torn and uneven.

These hairs are growing on a man's face. The hairs have been cut with a razor but have regrown. The short hairs would appear as stubble on the man's face.

Blood Clot

If you cut yourself, the wound will stop bleeding after a while. Your blood forms a clot that plugs the wound. The clot also stops harmful bacteria from getting inside the body and causing an infection.

Trapped cells

Pieces of blood cells called platelets arrive first at the wound. They glue together and plug the cut. The platelets also help a chemical called fibrin form threads over the wound. The threads trap more cells to create the clot. The clot then sets as a scab.

Clotting Conditions

Some people suffer from an illness called hemophilia. Their blood does not clot properly. If they cut themselves, the wound keeps bleeding. Sometimes blood clotting occurs inside the body. That is dangerous if it blocks major blood vessels.

When a blood vessel is cut, the liquid blood forms a solid blood clot. The blood clot is made up of red blood cells that are trapped in a mass of fibrin threads.

Food To Fuel

Food provides energy to fuel the body. To release the energy, the body breaks down food into simple substances. That is called digestion. Digestion starts when our teeth break food into small pieces. The food then passes into the stomach. The stomach breaks food into even smaller pieces.

A Long Journey

Most of the intestines are coiled up inside the body like a garden hose. The intestines lie just under the stomach, which is beneath the rib cage. If you stretched the intestines of an adult human into a line, it would be about 25 feet (7.5 meters) long.

In the intestines

The food then enters the intestines. There, chemicals break down the food into simple sugars. The sugars pass through the intestines into the bloodstream. The blood carries the sugars to fuel every part of the body.

The wall of part of the intestines is covered in bumps. The bumps increase the surface area of the intestines so more food can be taken into the blood.

Creating An Image

The human eye is like a tiny camera. A lens in each eye focuses light that bounces off objects in view. The light then falls on a sheet of cells at the back of the eye. The sheet is called the retina.

Rods and cones

The retina consists of two types of cells. Rod cells see in shades of light and dark. Cone cells see in color. Rods and cones gather the light that bounces off objects and send the signals to the brain. The brain then forms the picture that we can see.

Night Vision

Cone cells help us see in color, but they are not as good at seeing as rod cells. When night falls, the cone cells do not see as clearly as the rod cells. The eyes adapt for the lack of color and simply pick out shades of light and dark.

The cells on the retina at the back of each eye are either rod cells (pink) or cone cells (blue). There are far more rod cells than cone cells.

Natural Computer

The human brain is like a computer. It takes in signals from the outside world, such as sounds and smells. The brain then thinks about the signals and decides what to do. So, if you hear someone shouting "Move!" your ears send a message to the brain. The brain then sends a message to your legs to move.

Nerve Test

Test your nerves by catching a ruler. Hold out your hand with your finger and thumb apart. Get a friend to hold a ruler at the 0-inch mark. When your friend drops the ruler, catch it as quickly as you can. Note the inch mark where you caught it. The smaller the number, the quicker your reactions.

Sending messages

Messages are sent along special nerve cells called neurons. Neurons link every part of your body to the brain. For example, messages are sent to and from muscles through nerve cells called motor neurons.

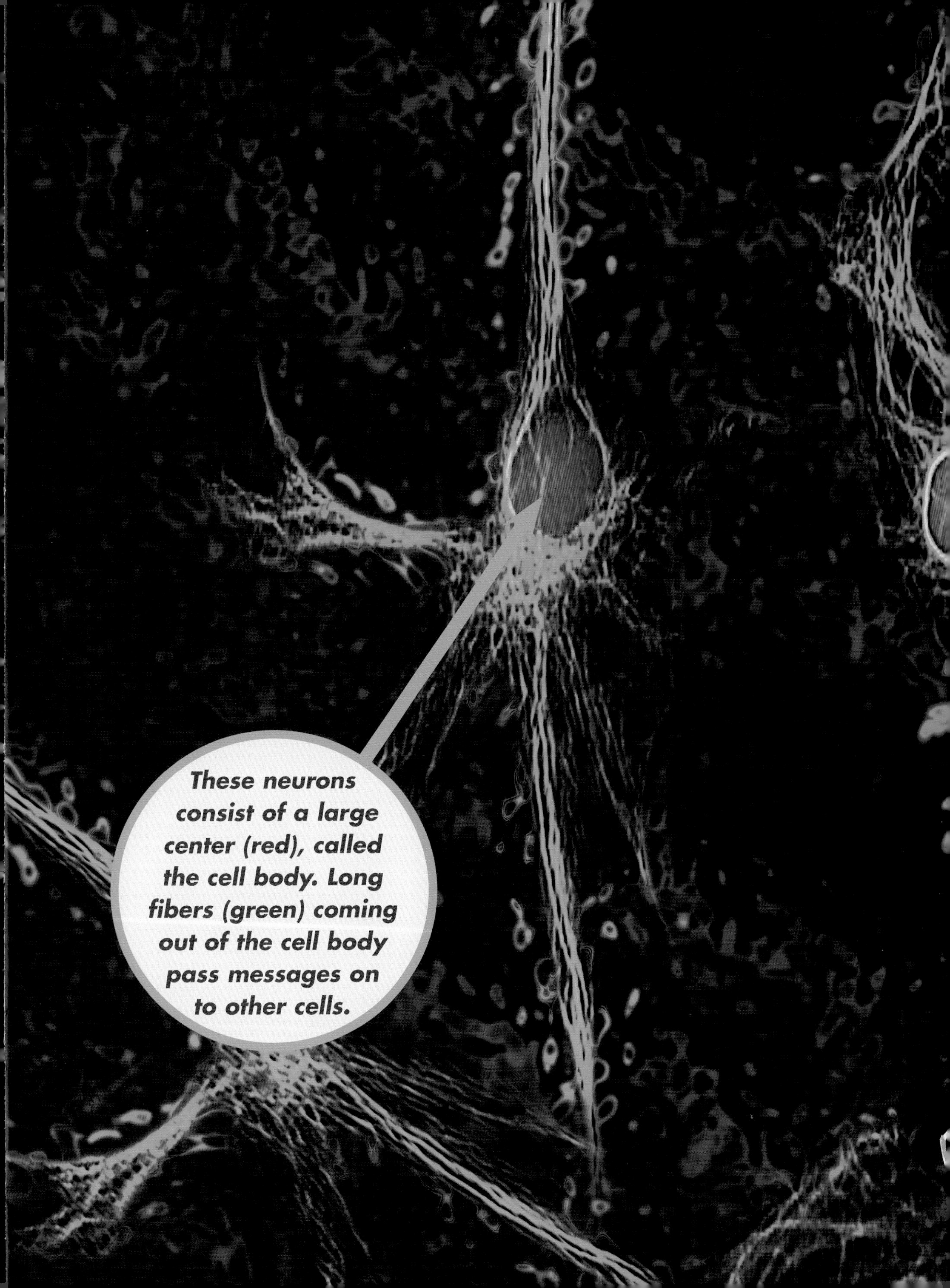

These neurons consist of a large center (red), called the cell body. Long fibers (green) coming out of the cell body pass messages on to other cells.

Glossary

bacteria: tiny, single-celled creatures that can be helpful or harmful to people.

cells: tiny building blocks that make up the bodies of all living creatures.

digestion: breaking down food into simple substances such as sugars, which the body can then use.

disease: something that stops the body of a living creature from working properly.

evaporate: to turn from a liquid into a gas.

fibrin: a body chemical that forms threads over a cut or graze. Fibrin helps scabs form.

follicle: tiny hole in the skin from which hair grows.

gland: a sac inside the body that makes a special liquid, such as sweat.

host: an animal or plant that provides a home for a parasite.

parasite: a living creature that lives and feeds on another living creature and causes it harm.

vaccine: an injection of dead viruses. Vaccines help the body fight off living viruses that attack cells.

viruses: tiny particles that live in the cells of living animals and plants. Most viruses are harmful and cause diseases.

Further Study

Books

Chandler F. *First Encyclopedia of the Human Body*. London, UK: Usborne Publishing Ltd., 2004.

Olien, Rebecca. *Human Body Systems* (various titles). Capstone Press, 2006.

Sweeney, Joan, and Annette Cable. *Me and My Amazing Body*. New York: Dragonfly Books, 2000.

Taylor-Butler, Christine. *Tiny Life in Your Body (Rookie Read-About Science)*. New York: Children's Press, 2006.

Ward, Brian R. *Microscopic Life in Your Body*. Mankato, Minneapolis: Smart Apple Media, 2004.

Web sites

www.kidshealth.org/kid
Filled with facts, activities, games, and experiments, this web site will help you find out everything you wanted to know about the human body.

yucky.kids.discovery.com/flash/body
Find out about human biology by looking at the gross and cool features of your body. Ask Wendell the Worm some yucky questions and he will provide the answers.

Index

GUITARS & BASS

Scott Witmer

Visit us at

WWW.ABDOPUBLISHING.COM

Published by ABDO Publishing Company, 8000 West 78th Street, Suite 310, Edina, MN 55439.
Copyright ©2010 by Abdo Consulting Group, Inc. International copyrights reserved in all countries.
No part of this book may be reproduced in any form without written permission from the publisher.
ABDO & Daughters™ is a trademark and logo of ABDO Publishing Company.

Printed in the United States.

PRINTED ON RECYCLED PAPER

Editor & Graphic Design: John Hamilton
Cover Design: John Hamilton
Cover Photo: Getty Images
Interior Photos and Illustrations: AP–pg 11; Fender Musical Instruments Corporation–pgs 3, 9, 18, 25, 26; Getty Images–5, 6, 7, 10, 15, 16, 19, 21, 23, 27; iStockphoto–pgs 1, 4, 6, 8, 9, 12, 20, 22, 25, 27, 28, 29; John Hamilton–pgs 8, 14, 17, 28, 31; Line 6, Inc.–pg 27; Marshall Amplification–pg 24; VOX Amplification USA–pg 27.

Library of Congress Cataloging-in-Publication Data

Witmer, Scott.
 Guitars & bass / Scott Witmer.
    p. cm. -- (Rock band)
 Includes index.
 ISBN 978-1-60453-691-1
 1. Guitar--Juvenile literature. I. Title. II. Title: Guitars and bass.
 ML1015.G9W64 2009
 787.87'19--dc22
                    2009006608

CONTENTS

Fender's Eric Clapton Signature Stratocaster guitar.

THE GUITAR

The guitar may be the most popular musical instrument ever invented. Who doesn't instantly recognize its distinctive outline? The guitar's unique sound ignites wild enthusiasm, and yet that sound seems infinitely diverse—the roaring rock power chord; the screaming Heavy Metal solo; the bright chords of country music; the complex notes of a jazz melody. The guitar symbolizes many things to many people.

The guitar has changed several times in its long history. It is closely related to ancient stringed instruments such as the lute. An early cousin of the guitar was the vihuela. It was used during the Renaissance in Europe, in the 16th and 17th centuries.

Over the years, the guitar's popularity increased because of its small, portable size and low cost. It was also easy to use for both single-note melodies or multiple-note chords.

> Today's guitars come in all shapes, sizes, and colors, from electric to acoustic.

Matthew Followill of Kings Of Leon performing during a rock festival on July 13, 2008, in Kinross, Scotland.

The guitar remained largely unchanged for many centuries. Then, in the 1930s, companies like Rickenbacker and Gibson began making electric jazz guitars. A huge jump in popularity came in 1951, when an American musician and inventor named Leo Fender released the Fender Telecaster. It was one of the first commercially produced solid-bodied electric guitars. Three years later, he released the Fender Stratocaster, and modern rock and roll was born. Even today, the Stratocaster is a favorite instrument of many musicians. It became so popular, so quickly, that today's models are nearly identical to that first model offered in 1954.

Today's musicians have many choices of guitars, from the acoustic masterpieces offered by Martin, to the popular electrics offered by Gibson, Fender, Rickenbacker, Ibanez, and Paul Reed Smith. Although the most popular modern guitars are made by American companies, foreign makers such as Yamaha also make fine instruments.

EVOLUTION OF THE GUITAR

Vihuela

Lute

Classical Guitar

Electric Guitar

Heavy Metal Guitar

Air Guitar

The Who's Pete Townshend playing a Fender Stratocaster in concert.

Most guitars include three main parts: the headstock, the neck, and the body. The headstock is where guitar strings are threaded through machine heads. These heads, or "tuners," are small pegs that allow the strings to be tightened or loosened. This changes the pitch of each string, allowing it to be

tuned to a specific note. Headstocks vary greatly in shape and design, but they all share the same function.

The neck of the guitar connects the headstock with the body. It is also where the fretboard is located. The fretboard contains several small metal

Fretboard

dividers called frets. The guitarist presses his or her fingers behind the frets to create different notes or chords on the guitar.

A guitar neck is usually made of wood. Many high-quality guitars use maple or cedar. Fretboards are often made of ebony, a hard, black wood. Inlays, or "place keepers," on the fretboard are commonly made of abalone, ivory, plastic, or colored wood.

The body of the guitar is where the sound from the vibrating strings is amplified, or made louder. This sound comes from the hollow body of the guitar when the vibrating strings echo through the sound hole. In an electric guitar, the sound is amplified, or made louder, by an electrical device called a pickup.

The body of the guitar also contains the bridge, which is where the strings are held. Bridges vary greatly in shape and quality, depending on the guitar's maker, and the personal preference of the musician.

Bridge

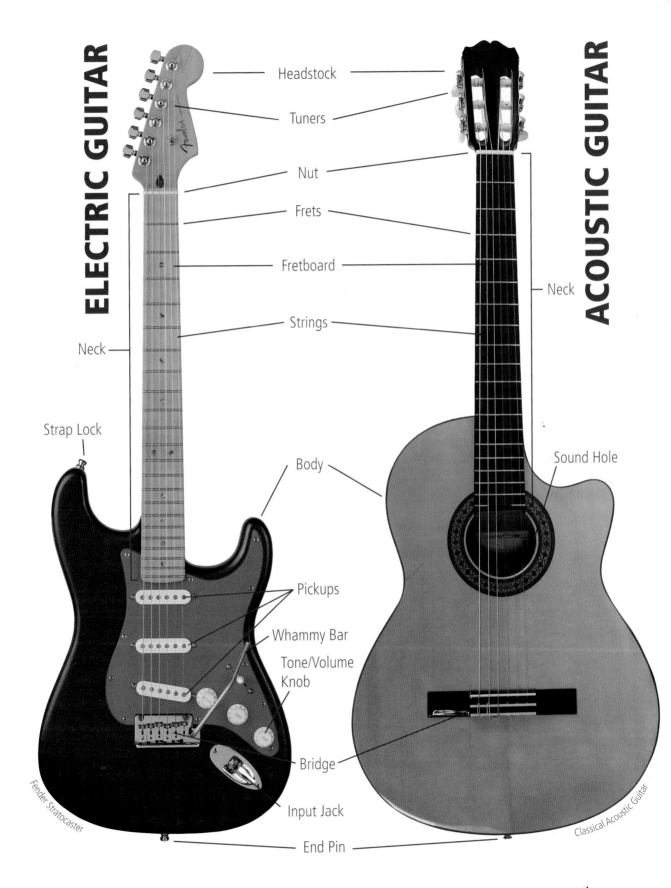

ELECTRIC GUITAR

ACOUSTIC GUITAR

Headstock

Tuners

Nut

Frets

Fretboard

Neck

Strings

Neck

Strap Lock

Body

Sound Hole

Pickups

Whammy Bar

Tone/Volume
Knob

Bridge

Input Jack

End Pin

Fender Stratocaster

Classical Acoustic Guitar

ACOUSTIC GUITARS

Acoustic guitars have been around for centuries. They remain extremely popular today. "Acoustic" means that they do not require electric amplification. They are extremely practical and portable instruments. Their unique sound is key to many kinds of music, especially country western and folk. Acoustic guitars can be found around campfires, accompanying impromptu sing-alongs, or in coffeehouses where singer-songwriters quietly perform. Many rock musicians compose their songs on acoustic guitars before recording in a studio with electric guitars.

The acoustic sound remains popular in today's rock music. Musicians often feature acoustic versions of their songs as "bonus tracks" on albums. MTV's popular show *Unplugged* features traditionally harder rock musicians playing their songs acoustically. Bands such as Nirvana, Korn, The Cure, and KISS have all traded in their electric instruments for acoustics to perform on the show.

Kurt Cobain of Nirvana playing an acoustic guitar on MTV's *Unplugged* in 1993.

Sheryl Crow playing an acoustic guitar in concert at New York's Rockefeller Center in 2008.

While most acoustic guitars are very similar, there are some different types. The classical guitar, often called the "Spanish guitar," has a much wider neck. Nylon strings are used in the three treble, or higher, positions. A classical guitar is almost always played with the fingers instead of a pick because of the lower tension and fragility of the nylon strings, and the wider spacing between them. Classical guitars have a softer, "warmer" sound than steel-stringed guitars.

Steel-stringed acoustic guitars are very popular today. They most closely resemble electric guitars, and are easy for beginners to play. They have a narrower neck, all six strings are steel (or a combination of brass, in some cases), and can be played with a pick. Steel-stringed acoustic guitars have a louder, "brighter" sound than classical acoustic guitars.

The kinds of wood and other materials used to construct acoustic guitars affect their tone, or sound. Many musicians insist on high-quality wood, like spruce or Indian rosewood, in the construction of their guitars. A leader in high-quality acoustic guitars is C.F. Martin & Co.

Acoustic guitars are crafted from different kinds of wood and other materials. The materials used in construction affect the tone, or sound, that a guitar makes. Martin is often considered the premier manufacturer of quality acoustic guitars. The company uses spruce, Indian rosewood, and decorative abalone inlays on some of its models. Other companies have begun using carbon fiber and plastic materials to construct their instruments. Some musicians insist that their guitars be made of a certain type of wood. Other guitarists can hardly tell the difference in sound quality. They choose their instruments for appearance and comfort. It all depends on the personal preference of the musician.

Another option for acoustic guitarists who play in traditional rock bands is the electric acoustic guitar. Acoustic electrics are sometimes designed to look like electric guitars. Their bodies have a distinctive "electric" shape, with a narrow profile and "cutaways" where the neck meets the body. Similar to standard steel-stringed guitars, electric acoustics have one or more electric pickups mounted on or inside the body of the guitar. Pickups transmit sound to an amplifier. This allows an acoustic guitar to be heard even in a band with louder electric guitars.

BUYING AN ACOUSTIC GUITAR

Acoustic guitars vary greatly in price. For musicians just starting out, less-expensive "beginner" guitars can be bought for about $100. As guitarists become more skilled, they can upgrade to higher-quality instruments. High-end guitars, like those made by Martin or Gibson, can cost several thousand dollars.

ELECTRIC GUITARS

If there's any single instrument that symbolizes rock bands, it is the electric guitar. Starting in the early 1950s, the electric guitar's popularity has become legendary, and shows no sign of fading.

In an electric guitar, the sound of the vibrating strings is captured by an electrical device called a pickup. Most electric guitars have between one and three pickups that can be switched on or off in various combinations to affect the tone of the sound. The pickup, which is usually an electromagnetic coil, sends an electric signal to an external electric amplifier, which generates a louder sound.

There are three main types of electric guitars: hollow body, semi-hollow body, and solid body. Solid-body guitars are the most popular electric guitars today. The body is a solid block of wood that vibrates very little and allows for a versatile tone and greater sustain, or continuous vibration of the strings. The solid-block design of the guitar makes it ideal for harder distortion-driven amplification. Famous solid-body guitars include the Fender Stratocaster and the Gibson Les Paul, plus many others.

HOW A GUITAR PICKUP WORKS

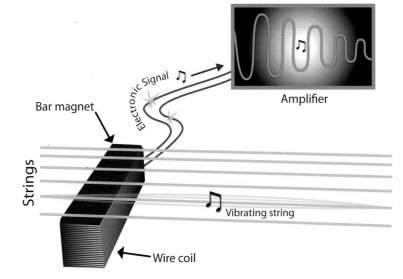

Bar magnet

Electronic Signal

Amplifier

Strings

Vibrating string

Wire coil

Guitar virtuoso Slash
performing live in New
York City in 2004 with
his Gibson Les Paul.

An Epiphone Casino hollow-body guitar, played by Noel Gallagher of Oasis.

Hollow-body guitars are light. They have a jazzier, brighter sound because their strings resonate throughout the entire body of the instrument. This gives hollow-body electric guitars a unique tone, which was once favored by John Lennon of The Beatles. The instrument is still preferred today by many rock musicians, including Noel Gallagher of Oasis. Examples of this type of guitar include the Epiphone Casino and the Gretch 6120.

 One of the most famous archtop, or hollow-body, guitars in history is the Epiphone Casino. John Lennon favored this guitar on The Beatles' early recordings. Some say that John Lennon purchased his first model because of his envy for Paul McCartney's Casino.

BUYING AN ELECTRIC GUITAR

Beginning guitarists shopping for their first instrument should consider buying an inexpensive model. Electric guitars can be found in many department stores for about $100, or slightly more for a package that includes an inexpensive amplifier. From there, prices increase to several thousand dollars, or even hundreds of thousands of dollars for rare collector's models.

The semi-hollow guitar is a hybrid of a solid-body and hollow-body guitar. Instead of a completely hollow interior, there is a block of wood that runs directly down the middle of the guitar body. In some cases, there are "sound chambers" built into a completely enclosed body. The semi-hollow interior allows the guitar to reproduce much of the unique tone of a full hollow-body instrument, while reducing amplifier feedback and increasing sustain. Examples of famous semi-hollow guitars include the Rickenbacker 300 series and the Gibson ES-335.

> Eric Clapton's Fender Stratocaster, which he named Blackie, sold at a 2004 charity auction for $959,500. This made Blackie the world-record holder for the most expensive guitar. Blackie was Clapton's favorite instrument. It was used on stage and in the recording studio between 1973 and 1985.

A detail shot of the author's Rickenbacker 330 semi-hollow electric guitar.

BASS GUITARS

The bass guitar is very similar to a standard guitar, but it uses thicker strings, which produce lower, deeper notes. A bass typically uses only four strings, although five-string basses are in limited use today.

Before the invention of the modern electric bass, bands used a fretless bass that was held upright. The instrument was difficult to play. It demanded the same kind of mastery as an orchestral instrument, like a violin or cello. However, in 1951, Fender Musical Instruments introduced the Precision Bass, the first commercially produced fretted electric bass. The frets made playing the instrument in tune much easier. Also, the electric pickups allowed it to be heard even in bands that used guitar amplification. The Precision Bass (commonly called the P-Bass) has remained largely unchanged since its release, which is proof of the design genius of the instrument.

Bass players are usually regarded as members of a rock band's rhythm section, like drums, and are relegated to the background. However, in recent years, several bass virtuosos have revolutionized the use of bass in rock music, bringing the instrument and its unique tone to the forefront. Highly skilled bass players today include Les Claypool of Primus, and Flea of The Red Hot Chili Peppers.

A Fender Precision Bass

Bassist Les Claypool at a concert in San Francisco, CA, in 2008. Legend has it that Claypool tried out for the heavy metal band Metallica after the death of the group's first bassist. Metallica's lead guitarist, James Hetfield, is said to have turned him down because he was "too good." Claypool went on to form the band Primus. Today, he is considered one of the best bassists to have ever played in rock.

OTHER STRINGS

The beauty of rock music today is that there is no limit to the diversity of your sound. Many bands have used "non-traditional" stringed instruments from time to time.

The mandolin (photo on facing page) is a fairly small guitar-like instrument. It commonly has four pairs of matched strings. This results in a very unique, "folksy" tone. The mandolin has been used by many bands, including Green Day, R.E.M., Dropkick Murphys, Led Zeppelin, and Panic! at the Disco.

The sitar is a long-necked, multi-stringed instrument that has been used since the Middle Ages. The rounded shape of the sitar's body creates a very unique resonating tone. Rock bands that have used the sitar include The Beatles, The Moody Blues, The Rolling Stones, and Tom Petty and the Heartbreakers.

The ukulele is another small, guitar-like instrument that is sometimes used in rock music. It is a traditional Hawaiian instrument. It is actually much like a very small version of a classical acoustic guitar, with vinyl strings commonly used. The ukulele has a very distinct "island" tone. It has been used in recent years by alternative artists that play Hawaiian-inspired music, such as Jack Johnson.

Ukulele

Sitar

Paul McCartney playing a mandolin at a concert in London, England, in 2008.

AMPLIFIERS

A pickup is an electronic device on an electric guitar that detects sound vibrations. When the strings of an electric guitar vibrate over the pickup, the magnetic coil inside generates an electric current. But the current, or signal, is much too weak to power a speaker. So, the signal is first sent to an amplifier, or "amp," to be processed. The amp boosts the signal electronically, and then sends it to a speaker, or set of speakers. The sound is now loud enough to be heard by an audience.

The first commercially available guitar amplifiers were built in the 1930s. In the 1950s, with the gain in popularity of the electric guitar, true advancements in guitar amplification began. Musicians discovered that by over-amplifying an electric guitar's signal, they could create new sounds and textures. The sound could be distorted. It could be made to echo, or reverb. The overall tone of a guitar could be completely changed simply by twisting a knob on an amplifier.

Carrie Brownstein of the rock band Sleater-Kinney performing in front of her two-amp stage setup at a 2005 concert in Los Feliz, CA. The amplifiers are tube models from American manufacturer Fender and British amplifier company Orange. Brownstein uses two different types of amps because of the unique tone she achieves with the setup.

As rock music's popularity increased in the 1960s and 1970s, amp manufacturers such as Fender, VOX, Marshall, and Mesa/Boogie experimented with maximizing distortion. New technology allowed musicians to adjust distortion levels at different volumes, or switch between distorted and clean tones with the push of a button or foot pedal. Today, these features are available in almost all amplifiers.

The premier amplifier of the time was Marshall. The company produced a high-gain stand-alone amplifier designed to be fed into another box that housed the speakers. This speaker box usually contained four 12-inch (30-cm) speakers (4x12). Guitarists often used two 4x12 speaker boxes and called it a Marshall "stack." The full Marshall stack (left) remains an iconic fixture on many rock-and-roll stages today.

The alternative to a stack is a "combo" amp (right). It is a single cabinet that houses the amplifier electronics and the speakers combined. Combos are very popular with working musicians because they are much easier to carry and load.

Originally, guitar amplification circuitry was a system that used a set of vacuum tubes, much like those found in old-time radios of the 1940s. These tubes required electronics and power supplies that were very heavy. They also became very expensive to repair as vacuum-tube technology became outdated. However, many serious guitarists swear by the tube amplifier's ability to produce warm, organic tones.

Vacuum tubes glowing in the chassis of a guitar amplifier.

In the past 20 years, as computer technology has become more advanced and less expensive, several manufacturers have replaced the tube circuitry with solid-state electronics. Non-tube amps can produce multiple tones and effects at a fraction of the cost. These amps are called "modeling" amps because they have the ability to mimic, or model, the tone and sound of tube amps. Roland and Line 6 were leading innovators in this field.

At first, "serious" guitarists scoffed at the claims of modeling amp manufacturers. They said they could easily tell the difference between a modeling amplifier and the real thing. However, as technology progresses, these amps sound more and more like "real" amplifiers. Today, many musicians have switched to solid-state electronic amps.

The advantages of solid-state amplifiers are clear: they are lightweight, inexpensive, and versatile. Because of these advantages, many manufacturers now offer hybrid tube/solid-state amplifiers. These devices use tube pre-amps and solid-state electronics in an attempt to capture the advantages of both technologies.

The debate between tube amps and solid-state amps continues to this day. There are many great arguments to be made for either side. For every musician who swears they can tell the difference, there is another who insists the amps sound the same. At the end of the day, the choice between a tube amplifier and solid-state amplifier is one of personal preference.

A Fender Cyber Twin SE combo amp, which combines tubes and solid-state electronics.

The popular rock band Weezer (left) does not even use amplifiers on stage! They use Line 6 POD guitar amp modelers (similar to the Line 6 POD X3 Pro, shown below) and plug right into a venue's sound system. At the end of the concert, instead of a 300-pound (136-kg) amp rig to haul around, they have a 5-pound (2-kg) guitar computer that sounds virtually the same.

Guitar amplifier prices vary widely. Entry-level amps can be found for under $100. There are even very small practice amplifiers that have no speakers at all. These versatile pieces of equipment are about the size of a deck of cards (below). They run on batteries, and have a jack to plug in

the guitar, plus a set of headphones. This type of practice amp can be very helpful to beginning guitarists, who must be considerate of others in their home when they are practicing.

High-quality amplifiers range from hundreds of dollars to several thousand. Much like guitars, there are very expensive collector's models that can sell for hundreds of thousands of dollars. In general, tube amps are more expensive than solid-state amps. The parts used to make tube amps are much more expensive.

EFFECTS PEDALS

Although modern amplifiers feature many ways to shape, mold, distort, and modulate sound, many guitarists crave more options. In the 1960s, companies began producing guitar effects pedals. These stand-alone devices add distortion, echo, flange, volume boost, and many other desired effects. The greatest advantage of effects pedals is that they are an inexpensive, ultra-portable way for guitarists to experiment and refine exactly what type of guitar tone they desire.

A guitarist using an effects pedal.

Effects pedals, also called stomp boxes, are most often small, battery-powered boxes placed in-line between a guitar and an amp. Many guitarists place several effects pedals next to each other. They can shape a guitar's tone by switching pedals on or off in any combination.

Perhaps the most famous of all effects pedals is the "wah-wah." Resembling a car's gas pedal, the wah-wah pedal lets a musician adjust a guitar's sound by rocking his or her foot back and forth. Technically, a wah-wah pedal is a band-pass filter that sweeps through a specific sound spectrum. Or, in layman's terms, it makes a guitar sound like a human voice saying the word "wah."

Also popular are distortion pedals, which mimic an amplifier playing at full volume. Many guitarists use fuzz distortion, which mimics an amplifier playing at full volume with torn, or "blown," speakers. In fact, before fuzz pedals came along, musicians would actually poke holes in the paper speaker cones of their amps to achieve this effect. A popular model of fuzz distortion pedal is the Electro-Harmonix Big Muff, which Kurt Cobain used during the recording of the Nirvana album *Nevermind*.

While most effects pedals are used to "dirty up" a guitar's sound, some are used to clean up and refine an instrument's tone. Equalizer pedals allow musicians to precisely refine the sound. Feedback reducers, noise suppressors, and volume limiters are also used to insure that an amplifier is getting the purest possible sound from a guitar.

In addition to stand-alone effects pedals, multi-effect pedal boards have recently become popular. Much like electronic modeling amps, multi-effect pedal boards can combine hundreds of effects together into one small package.

Effects pedals range in price from about $20 to upwards of $1,000 for multi-effect boards. Most pedals cost less than $100.

Effects pedals can be arranged on a pedal board. These setups can be very simple, or extremely complex. Jimi Hendrix, even though he revolutionized guitar sound in the 1960s, usually only used three effects pedals: a wah-wah, a fuzz distortion pedal, and an octave-changing pedal. Other musicians use many more pedals for a more complex variety of tones.

GLOSSARY

ACOUSTIC

When an instrument is played without electronic amplification to make the sound louder. The sound made by the vibrating strings of an acoustic guitar are made louder by resonating inside the hollow body of the instrument.

DISCO

A popular dance music with a strong bass beat. Disco was commonly heard in the 1970s.

DISTORTION

When the amplified signal from an electric guitar is "overdriven," which "clips" the signal and results in a kind of gritty, screaming buzz that is popular with hard rock musicians.

FEEDBACK

A loud, screeching noise that sometimes occurs in live concerts when electronic instruments are used, such as electric guitars. Sometimes called a feedback loop, it happens when an amplified sound from a loudspeaker is picked up by a microphone and the signal is amplified and then passed out again by the speaker. Feedback usually happens when live microphones are placed too close, or in the general direction of, the output speakers. It can be prevented by placing the speakers well away from the band or singers. In rock today, feedback is often deliberately used as a musical effect. It can be created by effects pedals, or even by guitarists shaking their instrument in front of an amplifier. Many groups have used feedback as part of their unique "sound," including The Beatles, Jimi Hendrix, The Who, and Nirvana.

REVERB

Reverberation, often called reverb, is when a sound continues to be heard even after the source has stopped producing noise. When a loud, continuous sound is created in an enclosed space (like a music hall), echoes can build up. When the instrument making the music stops, the series of echoes continue to bounce around the space, slowly decaying until they can no longer be heard. Reverb in rock music today is often used as a desirable effect, and can easily be produced with modern amplifiers.

SUSTAIN

The amount of time that a sound can be heard before it loses volume and becomes silent.

The Police performing at Met Center in Bloomington, MN, in 1982. From left to right: Stewart Copeland, Sting, and Andy Summers. Sting is playing a Steinberger headless bass.

INDEX